North American Indians Today

North American Indians Today

Apache

Cherokee

Cheyenne

Comanche

Creek

Crow

Huron

Iroquois

Navajo

Ojibwa

Osage

Potawatomi

Pueblo

Seminole

Sioux

DEC 1 4 2004

North American
Indians Today

Crow

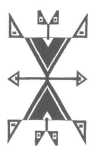

by
Kenneth McIntosh
and
Marsha McIntosh

Mason Crest Publishers

Philadelphia

We wish to thank all the wonderful people who helped us with this book:

Little Big Horn College, Dr. David Yarlott, Dale Old Horn, Tim Bernardis, Kevin Red Star, Jared Stewart, Jeanetta Wobig, Barney Old Coyote Sr., Winnie Old Coyote-Melkus, and the Rez Protectors: Lucretia Birdinground, Omney Sees the Ground, Brenett Stewart, Kimberly Deputee, Donna Falls Down

Mason Crest Publishers Inc.
370 Reed Road
Broomall, Pennsylvania 19008
(866) MCP-BOOK (toll free)

First printing
1 2 3 4 5 6 7 8 9 10
Library of Congress Cataloging-in-Publication Data on file at the Library of Congress.
ISBN 1-59084-669-9
1-59084-663-X (series)

Design by Lori Holland.
Composition by Bytheway Publishing Services, Binghamton, New York.
Cover design by Benjamin Stewart.
Printed and bound in the Hashemite Kingdom of Jordan.

Photography by Benjamin Stewart. Photos on pp. 10, 46, 57, 58 courtesy of Viola Ruelke Gommer; pp. 14, 18, 21, 24, 29 courtesy of Russell Maylone, curator of Northwestern University Library; p. 23 courtesy of Fort Laramie; pp. 51, 90 courtesy of the Hardin Boys & Girls Club; pp. 53, 86, 88, 89 courtesy of Lucretia Birdinground; pp. 55, 56, 60 courtesy of the Crow Nation Fair; pp. 65, 66 courtesy of Kevin Red Star; p. 76 courtesy of Joe Medicine Crow; pp. 17, 22, 47 Corel; p. 41 Artville. Picture on p. 6 by Keith Rosco.

Contents

Why is it so important that Indians be brought into the
"mainstream" of American life?
I would not know how to interpret this phrase to my people.
The closest I would be able to come would be "a big wide river".
Am I then to tell my people that they are to be thrown into the
big, wide river of the United States?

Earl Old Person
Blackfeet Tribal Chairman

Introduction

In the midst of twenty-first-century North America, how do the very first North Americans hold on to their unique cultural identity? At the same time, how do they adjust to the real demands of the modern world? Earl Old Person's quote on the opposite page expresses the difficulty of achieving this balance. Even the common values of the rest of North America—like fitting into the "mainstream"—may seem strange or undesireable to North American Indians. How can these groups of people thrive and prosper in the twenty-first century without losing their traditions, the ways of thinking and living that have been handed down to them by their ancestors? How can they keep from drowning in North America's "big, wide river"?

Thoughts from the Series Consultant

Each of the books in this series was written with the help of Native scholars and tribal leaders from the particular tribe. Based on oral histories as well as written documents, these books describe the current strategies of each Native nation to develop its economy while maintaining strong ties with its culture. As a result, you may find that these books read far differently from other books about Native Americans.

Over the past centuries, Native groups have faced increasing pressure to conform to the wishes of the governments that took their lands. Often brutally inhumane methods were implemented to change Native social systems. These books describe the ways that Native groups refused to be passive recipients of change, even in the face of these past atrocities. Heroic individuals worked to fit external changes into local conditions. This struggle continues today.

The legacy of the past still haunts the psyche of both Native and non-Native people of North America; hopefully, these books will help correct some misunderstandings. And even with the difficulties encountered by past and current Native leaders, Native nations continue to thrive. As this series illustrates, Native populations continue to increase—and they have clearly persevered against incredible odds. North American culture's big, wide river may be deep and cold—but Native Americans are good swimmers!

—Martha McCollough

Breaking Stereotypes

One way that some North Americans may "drown" Native culture is by using stereotypes to think about North American Indians. When we use stereotypes to think about a group of people, we assume things about them because of their race or cultural group. Instead of taking time to understand individual differences and situations, we lump together everyone in a certain group. In reality, though, every person is different. More than two million Native people live in North America, and they are as *diverse* as any other group. Each one is unique.

Even if we try hard to avoid stereotypes, however, it isn't always easy to know what words to use. Should we call the people who are native to North America Native Americans—or American Indians—or just Indians?

The word "Indian" probably comes from a mistake—when Christopher Columbus arrived in the New World, he thought he had reached India, so he called the people he found there Indians. Some people feel it doesn't make much sense to call Native Americans "Indians." (Suppose Columbus had thought he landed in China instead of India; would we today call Native people "Chinese"?) Other scholars disagree; for example, Russell Means, Native politician and activist, claims that the word "Indian" comes from Columbus saying the native people were *en Dios*—"in God," or naturally spiritual.

Many Canadians use the term "First Nations" to refer to the Native peoples who live there, and people in the United States usually speak of Native Americans. Most Native people we talked to while we were writing these books prefer the simple term "Indian"—or they would rather use the names of their tribes. (We have used the term "North American Indians" for our series to distinguish this group of people from the inhabitants of India.)

Even the definition of what makes a person "Indian" varies. The U.S. government recognizes certain groups as tribal nations (almost 500 in all). Each nation then decides how it will enroll people as members of that tribe. Tribes may require a particular amount of Indian blood, tribal membership of the father or the mother, or other *criteria*. Some enrolled tribal members who are legally "Indian" may not look Native at all; many have blond hair and blue eyes and others have clearly African features. At the same time, there are thousands of Native people whose tribes have not yet been officially recognized by the government.

We have done our best to write books that are as free from stereotypes as possible. But you as the reader also play a part. After reading one of these books, we hope you won't think: "The Cheyenne are all like this" or "Iroquois are all like that." Each person in this world is unique, whatever their culture. Stereotypes shut people's minds—but these books are intended to open your mind. North American Indians today have much wisdom and beauty to offer.

Some people consider American Indians to be a historical topic only, but Indians today are living, contributing members of North American society. The contributions of the various Indian cultures enrich our world—and North America would be a very different place without the Native people who live there. May they never be lost in North America's "big, wide river"!

According to Crow oral tradition, tobacco was the sacred seeds given to one of the Crow's earliest leaders. Traditional Crow Indians, along with many other Native Americans, still use tobacco to make their prayers. At the national powwow in Washington, D.C., this young woman demonstrates the way her people prepare tobacco leaves.

Chapter 1

The Great Migration

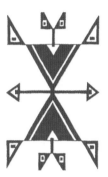

"Kahae sho' otdaachii?"
("Hello. How are you?" in the Apsaalooke language)

If you're like most people, you don't enjoy moving. It's a real hassle packing all your things. Saying good-bye to old friends is difficult. You wonder: Will I make new friends? Will I like my new home?

If you think relocating a family is difficult, how would you like to move an entire nation? Can you imagine generations of people spending their entire lives traveling from one home to another?

Southern Montana is home today for the Apsaalooke, the people commonly called the Crow. But they didn't always live in Montana. For sixteen generations, they have told and retold the *epic* of their travels. As they went from their ancestral homeland to the land promised them by the Creator, they crossed a third of the North American continent. Their journey lasted more than a century.

Originally, the Apsaalooke lived together with the ancestors of the Hidatsa people. They dwelled below Lake Superior and west of Lake Michi-

The Crow moved over much of the western United States in more than a century of migration.

gan, in what is today Wisconsin. They lived like other Indians of the Northern Woodlands, with permanent villages and advanced knowledge of agriculture.

One spring, this happy way of life ended. Hot winds blew continuously through the forests. The fertile soil became dry. Life-giving crops perished in the ground. Game animals disappeared. The people nearly starved. The leaders gathered for a council and hit on a lifesaving plan. Teams of fourteen hunters each were sent in different directions.

The eastward team returned hungrier than when they left. No large game animals had been found. Other teams soon straggled back with equally discouraging reports.

The team that had gone west did not return for a long time. When this last group did return, they brought back the most precious thing imaginable to starving people: each hunter sweated under a heavy load of dried buffalo meat. They reported traveling far to the West, to the place where forests gave way to immense rolling plains. At a passage between hills, the

"Crow" or "Raven" People

The Crow call themselves Apsaalooke. The word means "Children of the Large Beaked Bird." Indians of the Great Plains communicated between tribes with sign language. The sign for Apsaalooke was a flapping gesture, made with both hands. White people translated that as "crow," though it probably originally referred to the raven.

hunter had caught up with a vast herd of buffalo. They had trapped the rear of the herd, killing and butchering all they could possibly carry back to the people.

The tribe packed up and headed after the buffalo herds. They settled down in what is today southern Manitoba or northern Minnesota. Part of the tribe learned to live like the Indians of the high plains, dwelling in tepees and hunting buffalo. Others lived along a river in a more settled community, following their Eastern ways of fishing and farming. Around A.D. 1400, however, a combination of famine and conflict with other tribes forced them to move again.

A lake they named Sacred Waters was their next place of settlement. On the lakeshore, two chiefs—No Intestines and Red Scout—fasted and undertook sacred ordeals to know the Great Spirit's will. According to tradition, the Great Spirit gave Red Scout an ear of corn and told him to settle down there with his people. No Intestines was given a sack of seeds and told to go west. The proper way to use these sacred seeds would be revealed to the people when they reached their true home. No Intestines was also told his people would increase in numbers, becoming powerful and prosperous; eventually, they would live in a truly beautiful land.

The people moved again, and by 1450, they had reached the Missouri River. There, they moved in with the Mandans. These Indians lived in great lodges made of earth piled atop wooden frameworks. The Mandans were

The Crow arrived in a land with mountains, forests, and streams—everything they needed to live well.

The Good Country

"The Crow country is a good country. The Great Spirit has put it in exactly the right place; while you are in it you fare well; whenever you go out of it, whichever way you travel, you will fare worse. Everything good is to be found there. There is no country like the Crow country."

—*Arapooish (Sore Belly), speaking to a fur trapper, quoted in* The Adventures of Captain Bonneville, *written by Washington Irving in the eighteenth century.*

gracious hosts, and there was plenty of food, but No Intestines knew this was not the promised land of his vision.

Around 1500, No Intestines announced it was time to follow his vision and move westward. He said to his people, "It is time for me to follow the Great Spirit's instructions. I have waited too long. All who would like to come with me are welcomed."

Around four hundred of the people chose to go with No Intestines. Tearful good-byes were said to friends and loved ones who stayed behind. No Intestines' people walked off toward the sunset. By doing so, they began a whole new tribe. No longer would they live in settled lodges; now they were *nomads*. The members of this new group called themselves "Biiluuke"—"Our Side." All they had for guidance was a sack of sacred seeds and faith in the Great Spirit's promise.

The Crow's historians do not say how long they walked. Finally, the people came to a lake too large to see across and so salty its water could not be swallowed—what today we call the Great Salt Lake in Utah. From here, they traveled east. They came to a huge pit in the ground, roaring with fire. Historians today assume this was a burning coal vein, somewhere in the area of present-day Colorado or northern New Mexico.

Finally, around the year 1550, the community reached their promised land. No Intestines had long ago died. His apprentice, Running Coyote, had followed him as chief. The Apsaalooke finally reached the land for which they had been looking. Today's Yellowstone River flowed north of the land, and the Bighorn River went through it to the south. The Bighorn Mountains

The Crow people have followed a long road—and their road leads them forward into the future.

Worth Telling

"The story of our ancestors is truly great, exciting, and worthy of retelling from time to time. We have been here in our Mother-Earth-Land—which the Europeans have called America, the New World, the Western Hemisphere—for a very long time."

—*Joseph Medicine Crow*, From the Heart of Crow Country

The bison plays an important role in Crow traditions.

bordered on the east. It was temperate land, with varying seasons but none too harsh. The landscape also varied—from high mountains to river valleys, grassy plains to rolling plateaus. Plenty of buffalo roamed the plains. Truly, this was a good land, and here the people knew their journey to be at an end.

Chief Medicine Crow, in a picture taken by Edward S. Curtis in 1908. Medicine Crow was noted for his visions of the future, including the coming of the railroad and European cattle on the reservation. He led his people wisely as they were forced to adapt to the reservation way of life.

Chapter 2
Later History

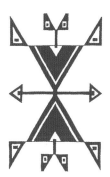

A thousand tepees stand proud and tall, white covers sprouting from the grasslands. Their poles point skyward above the smoke flaps, and streamers wave gaily in the breeze. A mounted procession clomps through the middle of the encampment. Men and women sit proudly atop strong horses bred for speed, agility, and beauty. Men wear eagle feather head-dresses, some with trailers flowing down their backs. Vests and bands covered with intricate beadwork attest to the great artistic skill of the people. Women ride in beautiful dresses, covered with elks' teeth. Later, as night falls, the thunder of a dozen drums fills the air. Rhythmic chants soar above the camp, prayers and pride for all to hear. Hundreds of moccasin-clad feet stomp and shuffle, feather **bustles** sway, and jingling metal cones chime on dancers' bodies.

This is the Crow Tribal Fair. The time is the third week of August, any year in recent memory. It could be much longer ago, though. The ceremonial attire, dances, and powwow camps of the Crow Indians today are a continuation of a lifestyle that began in this land three hundred years ago.

Around 1725, a Crow war party journeyed to Wyoming and took a stallion from the Indians there. The Apsaalooke people quickly experienced the wonderful advantage of horses for hunting and transportation. By trading, breeding, and stealing, they acquired many horses. Other Plains tribes used hammocks called *travois* to haul children and packs behind their horses when they moved camp. The Crows, however, had so many horses they could put children and leather bags on packhorses instead.

Bison (what we often call buffalo) provided most of the things the Apsaalooke needed to survive in their homeland. Meat for nourishment, hides for clothing and tent covers, and bone for tools all came from the bodies of these large shaggy creatures. A single bison can weigh two thousand pounds—plenty of meat on the hoof. When the Apsaalooke arrived in Montana, there was no shortage of buffalo; thirteen million lived in the state.

According to tradition, Chief Running Coyote developed an **ingenious** way to hunt the formidable bison. His technique was called the "buffalo jump." Parallel piles of boulders would be set up atop a bluff, leading to a steep drop off one end. Bison were spooked into running between the barriers, and in their panicked state they would run right off the edge. If they survived the fall, hunters beneath the cliff would kill them with narrow-tipped arrows. Women and children would skin the beasts and transport the meat back to camps.

The Crow, Sioux (Lakota, Dakota, and Nakota), Cheyenne, and other tribal nations were constantly bumping up against one another. Meetings could lead to trade, but they also frequently contributed to horse theft and warfare. War between the Plains Indian nations, however, was not the wholesale slaughter Europeans practiced. Few people died in Indian battles, and the gains and losses were counted in **prestige** and horses rather than occupation of land or destruction of villages.

The Crows value hospitality, so the first Europeans to meet them were greeted warmly and offered food and shelter. In the early 1800s, the U.S. government established a relationship with the Crow, using fur trappers as go-betweens. The fur trappers, popularly known as "mountain men," were sometimes badly maladjusted people living in the West because they got along poorly in their own culture. Nonetheless, trappers were welcomed in Apsaalooke villages.

The Crow are known for their continual friendly relations with the U.S.

Horses, which came to the Crow in 1725, transformed their way of life. Edward Curtis asked his subjects to dress in their regalia for this picture, taken in 1909.

Counting Coup

An important Crow war custom was counting coup. Crow warriors gained honor in this way. They could accomplish a coup four ways: touching an enemy in battle, stealing an enemy's horse, leading a successful war party, or taking an enemy's weapon. Warriors who had accomplished all four means of counting coup were eligible to become chiefs.

government. Although they were often treated unfairly by whites, the Crow kept their end of treaties with Washington. In 1851, the U.S. government offered the Apsaalooke what is now known as the First Treaty of Fort Laramie. This assigned the Crow more than 38 million acres (15.4 million hectares) in northern Wyoming, southern Montana, and western South Dakota. This treaty was not enforced for long. The Dakota, who had superior firearms, kept moving in and hunting on Crow lands, while the government troopers did little to stop them. When gold was found in Crow country, the government did nothing to prevent white miners from encroaching onto Crow lands.

Early in the 1860s, the Crow faced grave danger. The Dakotas sent messengers to the Northern Cheyenne and Arapaho to join them in attacking the Crow. One Arapaho chief was troubled by the idea of such destruction. He refused to fight and warned the Crow of the coming attack. The Ap-

The Crow hunted buffalo by driving herds over cliffs.

The first treaty between the Crow and the U.S. government was signed at Fort Laramie.

saalooke quickly pulled up stakes and moved their camps together on the banks of Pryor Creek.

On that fateful morning, 1,200 Crows faced an army of the Dakota and their allies that numbered between eight and ten thousand. All the enemy warriors held firearms while the Crow did not. The Crow were resourceful fighters, but they would need a miracle to prevail against such huge odds.

According to Crow tradition, they received just that. Fighting hard and aiming their arrows well, the Crow survived the first massive waves of attack. Then a courageous Apsaalooke warrior galloped out alone toward the enemy lines. Using sign language, he told them: "You are a mighty gathering. The Raven people will fight you in a great way today. We have two more bands coming, and then you will have a real fight on your hands!" He was bluffing, but at that point, an elk herd, stirred by the noise of battle, began milling around. The dust kicked up by the elks' hooves

The Crow fought other tribes to keep their lands along the Little Big Horn River.

looked to the Dakota like another army approaching. Incredibly, a herd of bison on the opposite flank of the Dakota army did the same thing—and was perceived the same way.

At this point, another wonder appeared. A rider on a painted horse, whom no one had ever seen, galloped down from the ridge and threw himself against the enemy warriors. It seemed bullets could not touch him. Both sides could only conclude he was a spirit warrior. Seeing their enemies' fear, all the Crow fighters charged into the opposing warriors. The Dakota, Cheyenne, and Arapaho broke ranks and scattered to their villages.

Despite this victory, the Crow were forced to make concessions when the government presented a new treaty at Fort Laramie in 1868. Pressured by white gold-seekers, government representatives reduced Crow lands to nine million acres. Forced to live in limited space, the Apsaalooke became vulnerable to disease. *Tuberculosis* and other illnesses devastated them. In their first decade on reservation land, three out of four Crow died from disease.

In 1876, Crow warriors were involved in the most famous fight of the American West—the Battle of Little Bighorn. The U.S. Army asked the Crow for *scouts* to help fight against their old enemies, the Sioux and Cheyenne. Five Crow warriors—White-Man-Runs-Him, Curly, Hairy Medicine, Mitch Boyer, and Goes Ahead—served under General Custer. The

Tepees, which could easily be broken down and pulled by horses, were ideal homes for buffalo hunters like the Apsaalooke. Today, they are used for camping out during the annual Crow Fair.

general wrote to his wife, "I now have some Crow scouts with me, they are magnificent looking men."

On June 25, the Crow scouts informed Custer that a massive Cheyenne and Sioux camp lay ahead of him. They told him the Indians were expecting the *cavalry* and urged him not to attack. Custer ignored their warnings. He commanded the Crow warriors to go home, and told them, "If we win this battle, you will be the noted men of the Crow Nation. If I die today, you'll get this land back from the Sioux and stay on it, happy and contented." Custer led his troops into a death trap, and the Crow scouts spent the day evading large groups of triumphant Sioux and Cheyenne.

From 1882 to 1884, the government again reduced Crow lands. Mineral deposits and railroad routes made the land valuable to whites, so the Crow were pushed back to the eastern portion of their reservation. Of the 38 million acres (15.4 million hectares) originally promised them by the United States, the Crow were left with slightly more than two million (810,000 hectares). This is the land they live on today.

In the twentieth century, the Crow faced new legal and cultural threats. The government outlawed some of their traditional practices—Sun Dances, sweat lodges, the *peyote* ceremony, and traditional songs. The government believed such "Indian doings" must be eliminated in order to help the Crow survive in the modern world. This *cultural oppression* was nearly as threatening as hostile enemies or smallpox had ever been.

In 1920, Crow land was divided up, or allotted, to individual families living on the reservation. Under the previous policy, land belonging to the

Longtime allies of the United States, the Crow assisted Custer in his campaign of 1876.

Today there is a memorial to troops of the Seventh Cavalry who died at the Battle of Little Big Horn. On June 25, 2003, a memorial was dedicated to the Sioux and Cheyenne who died in that battle. There is an annual reenactment of the battle on the site.

whole tribe could only be sold with the agreement of tribal leaders. Now, individual families could sell their land to whomever they wanted. Facing poverty, families would sell their land to non-Indian farmers. In this way, more than a third of Crow Nation land passed out of Indian hands between 1920 and 1962.

Along with loss of their good land, the Crow suffered the loss of their precious horses. White farmers complained for years about Crow horses wandering off Indian-owned land and into their fields. In 1919, the Secretary of the Interior ordered the Crow to kill off their horses. No one obeyed. So in 1923, the government paid gunmen to come up from Texas and kill Crow horses. The Crow's great herds were reduced to virtually nothing.

Today only the graves mark the battle of Little Big Horn.

Chief Plenty Coup worked for schools to be established on the Crow Reservation and encouraged his people to become educated in "white man's ways." At the same time, he held on to their traditional culture—setting a course that would benefit his people for years into the future.

Through the Great Depression of the 1930s, the Crow were fortunate to have Robert Yellowtail serve as superintendent of the reservation. Yellowtail got Yellowstone Park to donate bison for the reservation, and private horse owners donated breeding stock. **New Deal** programs were secured to help improve reservation forests and farmlands. Following a tradition of proud service in the armed forces, modern-day Crow warriors fought in World War II, Korea, and Vietnam.

The Supreme Court decided in 1981 that the Crow do not have the right to require licenses for fishermen using the Little Big Horn River. It was a serious loss for Indian land rights.

The last half of the twentieth century was a mixed bag of economic gains and losses for the Crow. In 1958, the tribe sold the Yellowtail dam site and reservoir to the U.S. government for $2.5 million. This issue bitterly divided the tribe, since it was fiercely opposed by the tribes' *traditionalists*. Nonetheless, the sale was a definite gain for the tribe's economy. In 1962, the tribe was also paid $10 million as compensation promised in the 1868 treaty. **Perseverance** in pursuing their land claims had paid off. The money was partially distributed to individual families and partly spent on land purchase and development.

These gains, however, were offset by the loss of rights to the Bighorn River in 1981. Until that time, the tribe had been requiring licenses from fishermen on the river that winds through their land. In a move that appalled **advocates** of Indian rights, the U.S. Supreme Court ruled that treaties with Indian nations did not include waterways on their reservations. This meant the tribe lost thousands of dollars of revenue each year from licensing fees.

Finally, in 1994, the Crow received settlement from another long-running dispute. In 1891, a government survey crew had made an error that reduced Crow boundaries by 36,000 acres (14,500 hectares). The land is valuable, since there are close to 100,000 tons of coal under each precious acre. The Bureau of Land Management agreed to compensate the tribe for the value of the land they had been shorted. An $85 million trust fund has been set up for use by the tribe.

For centuries now, the Crow have fought to enjoy their land. They have endured smallpox, hostile attacks from other tribes, and legal manipulation by a government they sought to befriend. The Crow have shown tremendous resourcefulness and adaptability. Today they are as strong as ever in the Good Country so long ago promised to them.

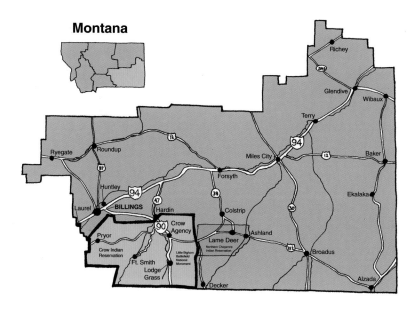

The Crow Nation today is in the southeast corner of Montana. It is a fraction of their original lands.

The Crow Tribal Government offices are the political heart of the Crow Nation.

Chapter 3

Current Government

PResident Carl Venne and members of the newly elected Crow Tribal Council know they have plenty of work ahead of them. In the United States, government-registered Indian tribes are treated as sovereign nations. Each tribe has the authority to choose its own leaders and make its own laws, providing these do not interfere with the laws and business of the federal government. The Indian Reorganization Act of 1934 ended many traditional tribal governments. The government urged tribes to adopt Western-style governments with a written *constitution* and elected officials.

The Crow were reluctant to abandon traditional ways of leadership, but in 1948 they did accept a written constitution. It created a unique form of tribal government—pure democracy. Article I simply stated: "The Crow Tribal Council shall be composed of the entire membership of the Crow tribe." It went on to state that the council (everyone) would elect a Chairman, Vice Chairman, Secretary, and Vice Secretary for the tribe.

The Council (all tribal members who wanted to come) met four times yearly and at special meetings if necessary. When issues were particularly important or emotional, hundreds would show up. Fans of the old system pointed out that everyone had a chance to be directly involved in tribal affairs. Opponents pointed to its *inefficiency*: it was very difficult to get that many people to agree on much. It was also *notoriously* changeable. The majority in one meeting might be a minority at the next. Programs and offices could be changed quickly. This apparent instability made some companies reluctant to do business with the Crow.

A political milestone was the May 12, 1990, election of Clara Nomee as Tribal Chairperson. She was the first female tribal leader. In her younger years, Clara struggled with harsh circumstances. Her mother and father both died in 1976, and she began drinking heavily. In 1977, she experienced a Christian conversion and found freedom from alcohol. In 1988, she was elected Tribal Secretary, and in 1990, Chairperson. She was reelected in 1994. During her administration, the boundary dispute with the government was settled, along with the large financial settlement to the tribe. She was also in office when the casino was approved. Her political career ended in *controversy*, but she clearly provided leadership that enabled the Crow to become stronger economically.

On July 14, 2001, the Crow adopted a radically new constitution. The constitution created a government with three branches, like the U.S. government. The executive branch consists of the Chairman, Vice Chairman, Secretary, and Vice Secretary. The legislative branch consists of eighteen legislators or representatives. Each Crow district has three representatives. The districts are: Pryor, Little Big Horn, Black Lodge, Center Lodge, Lodge Grass, and Wyola. Two representatives serve four-year terms, and one serves a two-year term. The Speaker of the House and Secretary of Legislature are chosen from these representatives. The judicial branch consists of Chief Judge, Associate Judge, and Appellate Judge.

Adoption of the new constitution did not come without controversy. After 53 years of doing things differently, the tribal council had been reduced from six thousand members to just eighteen. Many people felt they had lost political power. Those who favor the new constitution, however, point out its many advantages. They feel the new way offers more *accountability* and less *factionalism*. Advocates of the new constitution point out that it actu-

> "I may not be able to walk on water, but I can sure swim pretty good."
>
> —*newly elected Crow council member Jared Stewart*

Jim Ruegamer, Chief Judge for the Crow Nation in 2002.

ally ensures everyone a voice, whether their view is popular or not. Now there are public hearings and district meetings. Before, if you had an unpopular idea, you might not have been called on at the large council meetings. Some people also point out that votes will be more accurate under the new constitution than the old method of voting by voice, and votes are less likely to be bought.

Another current issue is land sales. Under the 1948 constitution, individual members of the tribe could sell their land. Over the years, 34 percent of the Crow Nation has been sold into non-Indian hands. Some of the new council members are hoping to halt that. Economic development has been stalled, and new council members see that as a key issue in 2003. Yet another item of concern is the worn-out sewer system.

Tribal government involves not only politicians but many people who work for the tribe. For example, Darren Cruzan is the chief of the Bureau of Indian Affairs Police Force on the Crow Reservation. When Becky Shay interviewed him for an article in the *Billings Gazette,* he described a tribal police officer's job as "90 percent boredom and 10 percent chaos." A small force of only twenty-one officers is responsible for safety and crime control in a nation spread over 3,500 square miles (about 10,000 square kilometers).

Crow Agency Public School has an enrollment of 270 students in kindergarten through sixth grade. Many of the students and teachers still speak the Crow language. Every September, the students and staff start off the school year celebrating Native American Week. Crow culture is included in the curriculum throughout the year.

The Crow/Northern Cheyenne hospital, with twenty-four beds, was opened in 1995. It is located on the Crow Reservation and serves both tribes.

Some of the tribal officers' jobs are ordinary and routine. For example, traffic rules must be enforced. Officer T. R. Littlelight visits the reservation schools weekly to teach GREAT—Gang Reduction Education and Training. But tribal police officers also must deal with the same sorts of heartbreaking issues faced by their comrades throughout the nation. They have to step into family situations where child abuse or wife beating takes place. They arrest people who are drunk or high on methamphetamines or marijuana. Tragically, they sometimes have to respond when drunk driving leads to death on reservation roads.

In this new millenium, Crow politicians and police officers are working hard to improve the lives of their people. Using new techniques, they hope to preserve the successes and improve the failures of years past. The new ways may seem to be on shaky ground now but they also offer great hope for the future of the Crow.

Many people in the Crow Nation belong to Baptist, Catholic, or Pentecostal churches.

Chapter 4

Today's Spiritual Beliefs

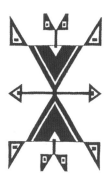

Sue sits in the fourth pew of the small church, listening intently as she cradles a baby in her lap. She is young—not yet twenty—but she has already seen too much of what the world can do. The speaker is sharing his testimony, relating what God has done in his life.

He tells how he got off to a rough start. He never knew his father. He became addicted to drugs, dropped out of school, and didn't have much to live for—until he fell in love with a girl. They married, and at first things went well, but then he fell back into the drugs. That's when a friend invited him to this church. "It's been almost a year now that I've been freed from the drugs. I have a new baby boy, and my wife and I are happier now. I owe it all to Jesus—and this church."

Sue smiles. The young man is her husband, and she is as grateful as he is for the changes this Pentecostal church has brought into their lives.

Joe sits in the dark, sweat pouring from every pore of his naked body. The tarp-covered lodge fills with moist heat. A man beside Joe hands him a hand-rolled cigarette, and Joe blows prayers to the Creator. His mind leaps back to the events of his life that keep him coming here.

He was proud to serve in Vietnam, yet he returned home with mental wounds. Bad dreams woke him at night, and he had terrible headaches during the day. The doctor in Billings gave him medication, but that made things even worse. He felt like his brain was snowed under a fuzzy weight.

He shared his troubles with an older neighbor, a man said to have great spiritual power. The neighbor invited Joe to join him in the sweat lodge, a religious practice that is no longer banned by the U.S. government. Joe had gone to college in the city, where they made fun of such Indian ways, but as the prayers of his elders ascended with smoke, he felt something he'd never experienced before. That night, he slept like a baby for the first time in years.

Now he lives each day connected to the Creator. Wholeness and health have been given back to him, thanks to the Creator and the traditional ways of his people.

For many Crow people, religion is a private matter, something they would prefer not to share publicly. Religion plays an important role in their lives, however. Sue and Joe are fictional characters—yet they both represent spiritual practices common to today's Crow Indians.

The majority of the Crow are Christian. Catholic, Baptist, Latter Day Saint, and Foursquare Gospel denominations have churches on the reservation. The largest and most active churches are Pentecostal. Pentecostal churches tend also to be Evangelical; that means they emphasize the Bible as God's literal written words, and Bible-based sermons are part of each service. Pentecostal worship focuses on direct experience of God's Spirit. Worshipers may speak in "tongues"—*ecstatic* speech that resembles foreign languages. Services are emotional and lively. Evangelical and Pentecostal churches emphasize the need for people to have a personal relationship with Christ. They stress the power of such conversions to change lives and overcome destructive habits. Drinking and smoking are discouraged.

Although Christianity is common on the reservation, many Crow also continue to believe and practice their religion in the traditional way. For a century, they had to keep these beliefs underground for fear of punishment

Many North American Indians see tobacco much differently from other North Americans. Native people believe that tobacco was enslaved by the tobacco industry's legalized drug trade—when the plant was meant by the Creator to be used in ceremonial meditation and prayer. This artist's rendition of a man wrapped in a blanket is intended to symbolize the old "tobacco songs"; the feather indicates the presence of great spiritual power.

from white government agents. The past few decades, however, have seen a **renaissance** of openly practiced Crow spirituality.

Dale Old Horn is department head of Crow studies at Little Big Horn College. He is a tall man, with long gray hair pulled back into a ponytail. His voice is deep and full, which may be one reason he is sought after to *emcee* at powwows across the country. He is both friendly and confident as he explains traditional Apsaalooke beliefs.

There is one God, Dale explains. God is **omnipotent**, creating both good and evil. The Crow word for God is both male and female, not "He." God gives humans spiritual knowledge to choose between good and evil; the choices we make in life decide whether our lives will be happy or miserable. The afterlife is the same for all, since all are children of God.

An important Crow concept is spiritual agency. This may be compared to the Christian view of communion, where bread and wine carry God's presence to participants. The Apsaalooke believe the power of God is found not only in a ceremonial substance like communion's bread and wine but in all of creation. Each aspect of reality is a "spiritual agent" for God.

According to Crow beliefs, God is much greater than anything we can imagine or conjecture. Dale remembers his great-grandmother praying: "Creator, you who created things we can see and can't see—you have created things that we can understand and things that we can't understand. That is your power."

God placed his power in seven entities: heavens, air, fire, water, earth, plants, and creatures (including us). Having placed his power in these entities, God is careful about who experiences spirituality and what levels of spirituality. Not everyone will look at reality and see spiritual meaning, but those who understand spiritual agency will experience the spiritual world in the ordinary world around them. All things that we can experience with our senses could be spiritual blessings to us, say the Crow—if God wills it.

The Crow show their faith by means of personal sacrifice. When they participate in the Sun Dance, they give up food and water. In the sweat lodge, they endure intense heat. For the peyote ceremony, they give up food. Sacrifice shows faith.

The Crow have some ceremonies that are also common among other Plains Indians, such as the Lakota and Cheyenne. One such custom is the sweat lodge. The lodge is a small round enclosure made of sticks covered with burlap. Heated rocks are placed in the middle, and water is poured over the rocks. A flap covers the door, which is opened to relieve the heat between sweats.

Much symbolism is connected to the Crow sweat lodge. During the ceremony, the door flap is raised four times. Each time the door is raised a

42 *North American Indians Today*

Medicine Wheel and other sacred sites are located in the Big Horn Mountains. Traditional Crow are concerned that development of such sites may make it impossible for them to worship as they wish.

prayer is expressed. The sweat not only shows devotion to the Creator; it also purifies the body by removing harmful substances. If done improperly, the Crow believe the sweat lodge may cause physical harm. This has happened, says Dale Old Horn, when non-Indians have attempted to perform sweat ceremonies without proper knowledge.

The Sun Dance is practiced by most of the Montana tribes. Ceremonies are very sacred, and non-Indians are usually not allowed to attend. A large Sun Dance lodge is constructed out of upright poles connected by pole rafters to the large central pole. The buffalo is a central focus of the Sun Dance, along with the sun; the bison was the source of things needed for life, and the sun is the center of wisdom. The dances take place for three days and nights. During the ceremony, dancers go without food or water. Participants experience tremendous power from the ceremony.

The Native American Church came to the Crow from tribes in Oklahoma. This church's ceremonies center on the *sacramental* use of peyote, a small, spineless cactus that grows in Mexico and Texas. The Native American Church teaches brotherly love, care for family, self-reliance, and avoidance of alcohol.

The Crow do not participate in the Ghost Dance, which was once common to nearby tribes. According to Dale Old Horn, the Ghost Dance involves calling on the devil, and the devil is a concept foreign to the Crow.

A ceremony unique to the Crow is the Tobacco Dance. Many Tobacco Dance societies once existed, but only two remain today: the weasel and otter societies. Tobacco was the sacred seed given to No Intestines when he was given his vision of a future homeland for the Apsaalooke people (see chapter 1).

An important concern for traditional Crow people is preservation of sacred sites. Since the earth is a means of sacred agency, special places can impart spiritual reality in unique ways. One such place is Medicine Wheel, located high in the Bighorn Mountain, on traditional Crow lands. This is an enormous rock formation, arranged like a wagon wheel. Archaeologists are unsure who made it or why, but it has been a place of spiritual power for the Crow and other Montana Indians for generations. Many travelers come to visit the site, and much debate exists over ways to accommodate

"It is generally held by political scientists that native cultures are the basis and foundation of any nation of the world. By a new-found pride in native Apsaalooke culture, the Apsaalooke can ensure a strong, positive, secure, and prosperous future. And the Apsaalooke will live on in their beautiful culture—to be admired by all people as a nation in its true sense."

—*Dale Old Horn and Timothy McCleary,* Apsaalooke Social and Family Structure

This painting by world-famous Crow artist Kevin Red Star is titled Two Crow Brothers Waiting to Hot Dance. *The hot dance was traditionally performed by members of the warrior societies for the benefit of the tribe.*

Powwows give Native people around the country the chance to celebrate their cultural traditions. Powwow dances are not sacred. Sacred dances like the Sun Dance are only for those who have been carefully initiated.

In 1971, The Crow Tribe acquired a herd of 400 buffalo. Today they have the largest buffalo herd in Indian Country, exceeding 1,500 head. The Crow word for buffalo is Bi'Shee. *The buffalo are still culturally and spiritually important to many Plains Indian people.*

the wishes of tourists versus the need of Native people to practice their faith at Medicine Wheel.

The beliefs of today's Crow people resist stereotyping. Some Crow worship as their ancestors did, others use ceremonies borrowed from other Indians, and some follow the teachings of Christianity. In all their various forms, however, Crow spiritual beliefs give meaning, strength, guidance, and comfort throughout life. Whether they pray in churches, sweat lodges, or peyote rituals, many of today's Crow Indians are deeply spiritual people.

Barney Old Coyote, Jr. and his granddaughter Carrie Mariah Old Coyote-Melkus. Grandparents, aunts, and cousins are very important in the lives of today's Crow children.

Chapter 5

Social Structures Today

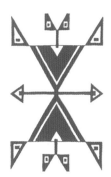

Jeanetta Wobig is the unit director at the Hardin Boys & Girls Club. She spends her life at the club, either with the kids or doing upkeep on the club building. An enrolled Crow, Jeanetta grew up in Lodge Grass. Her father was Indian, her mother Anglo. She lives with her husband and grand-daughter, and all three are involved in some way with the club. You can tell by the excitement in her voice that she loves her kids and her work.

Jeanetta works hard on several fronts for the boys and girls. She spends much time working with the kids daily and also does fund-raising. As stated on the club's Web site, "The goal of the Boys & Girls Club is to strengthen children's ability to believe in themselves through promoting healthy life choices. . . . This means promoting culture, drug awareness and abstinence, alcohol abuse prevention and open dialogue between the Native and Non-native club members."

This year the Boys & Girls Club had an art show for their parents. Many

Native children are wonderful artists and doing something like this helps build their self-esteem. Afterward, the parents enjoyed a reception with punch and cookies.

Through activities like this, Jeanetta encourages children's creativity, but she also stresses the importance of work and wise choices. She had the kids working on a project on the reservation picking up trash. The club implements another program called Smart Moves, an antidrug and alcohol program.

Since Jeanetta was a schoolteacher for many years, education is very important for her. Jeanetta and her high school helpers give the children help on their homework. Ten computers and an Internet satellite dish, given by the Boys & Girls Clubs of America, are a big help to the children. The Crow club was one of only a hundred across America that received the award.

Jeanetta also spends many hours fund-raising. A $5,000-grant was awarded the Crow club while Jeanetta was Executive Director. To help raise money for a new teen center, Jeanetta and helpers raised $800 flipping burgers at a concession stand during the Crow Fair.

When asked about her hopes for the future, Jeanetta tells of her desire to add on a teen center to the Boys & Girls Club, since there is no place in Hardin for teens to hang out. She wants to have a place where kids can come and do homework, where there are computers, tutors, a pool table, and snacks—and she also wants to provide them with a place where they can relax and talk, somewhere they might want to go after a prom event or for a New Year's Eve party. She wants to put some teens in charge of the project, so they can be the ones to design the center and set it up.

Caring people like Jeanetta can have a great positive impact in the lives of Crow youth. At the same time, the importance of the Boys & Girls Club reflects how many things have changed from the way they once were in traditional Crow culture. In times past, children would have learned all the necessary life skills from their elders. Most of their time would have been spent with clan members. As Dale Old Horn puts it, "Because of the loss of culture, many of the practices of the Apsaalooke people are being replaced by a tremendous amount of dysfunctional behavior." One aspect of this is the lessening role of family and clan in the social formation of teenagers. Organizations like the Boys & Girls Club can help fill the gap that was once filled by the clan.

Traditionally, Crow children were not only close to their parents and

Cherish Stops is a proud participant in the Hardin Boys & Girls Club art show.

Preston Bell and Aaron Fitzpatrick enjoy a snack at the Boys & Girls Club.

"...I hope that I can save my grandchildren. But times have changed so fast that they have left me behind. I do not understand these times. I am walking in the dark. Ours was a different world before the buffalo went away. ..."

—*Pretty Shield, Crow medicine woman, reflecting on the condition of tribal families in 1932*

siblings but also to their grandparents, aunts and uncles, and cousins. Clans are groups of related families. The Apsaalooke word for clan is *ashammaliaxxiia*, which means, "a lodge where the wood intertwines," a **metaphor** for the unity of the clan. The important role of extended family gave extra strength to the nuclear family.

Family is still vitally important for the Crow today. Winnie Melkus, a Crow mother and college student, says: "Family is your wealth. One member of a Crow family may be a drunk but the family will still care for that person and provide for him. They will provide food and necessities, but not alcoholic drink. He is still included in the family." The Crow language has no word for cousin or aunt; instead, Winnie's sisters are called "mother" by her kids—Mother Jackie, Mother Sara, and so on. Their cousins are called brother or sister.

Primary clan membership comes from one's mother. The mother's clan is responsible for the physical and emotional needs of the child. The father's clan is responsible for providing prayers of blessing and for reporting on a child's achievements before the rest of the tribe. According to Dale Old Horn, when he founded the clans, Old Man Coyote told the people: "No matter how poor, no matter how pitiful, no matter how unaccomplished your clan father may be, whatever he says on your behalf to the spiritual realm will come true." The father's clan also provides a child with "teasing cousins." This means if your fathers belong to the same clan, then you have free license to tease each other in public or in private.

Lucretia Birdinground poses in her elks-tooth dress. Like many teens, she realizes both the value of modern education and of her Crow heritage.

People on the Crow Nation live in frame or manufactured houses. Affordable housing is a problem on the reservation.

Although clan relationships are eroded by twenty-first-century culture, the Crow Tribal Fair is an event that helps tie people to their traditions, and to one another. The Apsaalooke word for this event is *Um-basax-bilua*, "where they make noise." The fair began in 1904, when Indian agent S. C. Reynolds was trying to get the Crow more interested in farming. He suggested they hold a fair, like the country fairs held in most communities around the country, where they could compete and show off their vegetables and cattle. To create more enthusiasm, Reynolds suggested they could hold traditional dances and ceremonies. This was an exception to the suppression of Crow ways at this time, and the tribe responded enthusiastically. Over the years, the agricultural aspects diminished and the social and cultural focus grew.

Today, the fair is a six-day event, held the third week in August just outside Crow Agency. During these six days, the Crow Nation becomes "Tepee Capital of the World" as more than 1,500 of these traditional Plains Indian shelters are set up along the Little Bighorn River. A 200-foot (61-meter) round dance area is the heart of the camp.

The event begins with a parade of brightly outfitted people on horses, and floats, in cars and trucks. The offer of cash prizes encourages a good turnout for this parade. The all-Indian rodeo and horse races follow. Throughout the afternoon, dances are held.

The dances begin with a grand entry. An honor guard of flag bearers, who are military veterans, leads the entry. This reflects the tradition of the warriors leading the people. Then, men's traditional, fancy, and grass dancers follow. Women's traditional, fancy, and jingle dress dancers come next.

There are several categories of powwow dances. Intertribal dances are spectator participation events, and exhibition dances are an opportunity for each tribe to display its traditions. Contest dances are judged and cash prizes given.

One category of competition is traditional dances. Male traditional dancers wear feather bustles, bone breastplates, and fur or feather head-dresses. Women traditional dancers perform in beaded and fringed buck-skin dresses, with fur braid wraps and eagle feathers in their hair. Both men and women traditional dancers move with deliberate steps and a proud attitude. Each of their movements has significance.

Young and old enjoy riding in the Crow Nation Fair parade.

Fancy dances are a recent custom. Fancy dancer outfits are wildly bright, with dyed feather bustles and shiny cloth outfits. Participants show off their athletic skills and timing.

The Crow Fair is an important social occasion for the Apsaalooke. A quarter of the ten thousand Crow Indians live off the reservation, so Crow Fair is a time for returning home, renewing acquaintances, and family ties. It is an opportunity for laughter, talk, and games.

The hand game, played by two opposing teams, is a traditional pastime that is still popular with today's Crow. A member of one team hides an object—either a stick or a bone—in one hand or the other. The opposing

The Crow Nation Fair begins with a parade of horseback riders, cars, trucks, and floats. There are cash prizes for the best entries.

Powwows like the one at the Crow Nation Fair help instill pride in each new generation of Indians.

Fancy dances, featuring bright outfits and dyed feathers, are a modern custom.

In the old days, the snowy wintertime was storytelling season for the Crow people. Children would sit around their older relatives and listen. These stories passed on the history and beliefs of the Crow, and also imparted valuable lessons—practical wisdom that shaped character and prepared young people for life. As the storytellers spun their stories, they would pause now and then and say, "Of course, no good Crow man or woman would do that," or "This was the right thing to do." Their listening audiences would all say "Eh!" to signal agreement. After the storytelling, tea and pudding would be served. The extended family would then discuss the stories, what they meant to them, and what their favorite parts were.

Edwina "Winnie" Old Coyote-Melkus enjoys horses, just as generations before and after her have done.

Rodeo competition is challenging fun for all ages.

Crow Clans

Apsaalooke tradition relates how, in the course of their journeys, the tribe came across Old Man Coyote. He said to them, "I am a member of this clan." The people replied, "What is a clan?" And he told them, "A clan is when people are related. You are not to marry within your clan."

There are ten clans among the Crow today:

Whistling Water
Bad War Deeds
Greasy Mouth
Sorelip Lodges
Big Lodge
Newly Made Lodge
Piegan
Filth Eaters
Ties the Bundle
Brings Game Without Shooting

team has to guess which hand. If they guess right, they get to keep the stick. There are fourteen sticks or bones, and when a team has lost all its sticks, the game is over. Teams may have anywhere from ten to forty members. As the other side prepares to guess, members of a team will chant, drum, and shake rattles. Thousands of dollars may be bet on a game.

Another traditional form of recreation is the arrow-throwing game. Two opposing teams of men play this game. The object of the game is to throw large arrows as close as possible to a previously thrown target arrow. Arrow-throwing tournaments take place during the summer, with competition between the six districts of the reservation.

The most popular sports on the reservation today are modern. Long noted for their expertise as horsemen, the Crow have many excellent rodeo riders. Basketball is also immensely popular, especially at the level of high school competition. Although these games lack traditional roots, they help to bind the tribe together into a cohesive and meaningful unit.

Jared Stewart, musician and Crow tribal councilman.

Chapter 6

Contemporary Arts

Jared Stewart is doing something a lot of people dream of—making a living playing his guitar. A happy thirty-something with a pleasant face and long ponytail, Jared fronts a "hot-rockin' blues" band. He has won numerous awards and played with big-name bands, an impressive achievement for someone who didn't pick up a guitar until he was nineteen. It's taken a lot of work to get to this point, though.

In high school, Jared was into sports and other school activities. He was twice a state champion in basketball. Then he discovered that music was what he really loved. At the beginning of his musical career, he would often call a place trying to line up a gig—and would be rejected. He didn't give up, though. He kept at it and stayed focused on his goal. Sometimes he only played for the bartender and an empty room. Yet he still stayed positive. He would say to himself, "Well, I'm on a bigger stage, in a bigger room than I played in last time. Eventually, people will catch on." Now, the Jared Stewart Band travels to play in Billings, Albuquerque, and Denver. It's a lot of work setting up and taking down the band's equipment, but Jared says they still play as hard for an audience of five people as they do for five hundred. He believes in giving his all.

A highlight in Jared's musical career was setting up the first Crow Native Day concert in June 2000. He took out a loan on his pickup truck to raise $12,000 for the event. With that, he brought his favorite artist, reggae singer Jimmy Cliff, to perform at the concert. The Jared Stewart Band also played. The event raised enough money to pay most of the bills, but in the end, Jared lost $4,000. Looking back, he says it was worth every penny. It was just great to be on the same stage as Jimmy Cliff and see all the people having a great time singing along with his songs.

With so much exposure in the area of Crow Nation, Jared tries to send a positive message to kids. He goes to schools and talks about being drug and alcohol free. He tells them, "I have to show you as much respect as possible because you'll be the leaders someday. Don't just settle for what you are now—live out your dreams. And be sure to brush your teeth—no one will listen to you if you don't." He explains later: "You have to be funny and talk on their level."

Before July 4, 1994, Jared was in trouble many times because of his drug use. He says, "I've been around the block a few times. That's the way it is here—there's a lot of despair. People say: 'Why should I get a job, I don't have a car?' Then they say: 'Why should I get a car, I don't have a job?'" Jared has been drug free since 1994 and believes his example can be a more powerful positive influence for kids than anything he could ever say. Jared is just one example of artistic talent in today's Crow tribe.

Kevin Red Star is a famous Crow painter. He draws on historical and modern subjects from his culture for inspiration. By exaggerating features and emphasizing the eyes of his subjects, he captivates the viewers' attention. His paintings are displayed in the Smithsonian Institution, Denver Art Museum, and museums in Belgium, China, Germany, and Japan.

Kevin was born in Lodge Grass, Montana, on the Crow Reservation, the third oldest in a family of nine. His parents were both artistically inclined. In 1962, he began formal art education at the Institute of American Indian Art. He learned to use various media and techniques from the finest Indian teachers. In 1965, Kevin won a scholarship to the San Francisco Art Institute. There, as a freshman, he won the Governor's Trophy for outstanding achievement. He also has studied at Montana State University in Bozeman and Eastern Montana College in Billings. Today, he is regarded as a master artist.

World-famous artist Kevin Red Star says, "I love the country and I love my horses." This life-sized painted pony will be auctioned to raise money for charities.

Many elements of Crow culture are represented in Kevin's paintings. Some portray powwows, or the use of the peace pipe for prayer, or a woman's elk-teeth–decorated dress. Though his subjects are traditional, he never stops growing in his techniques as an artist.

Earl Biss, who died in 1998, was another important Crow painter whose works also hang in museums worldwide. Raised on the Crow Reservation, he caught rheumatic fever at age eight and had to stay home from school. His father had him enrolled in art classes, and his skills in oil painting developed rapidly. He studied at the Institute of American Indian Art and San Francisco Art Institute. He also studied in European art centers like Amsterdam and Rome. His oil paintings use warm earth tones and rich texture. He portrays traditional Indian subjects but does so in an *impressionist* style.

The Crow tradition of fine arts is continuing strong into the new century. For example, sixteen-year-old Leon Sylvester Take Horse won first place in the 2002 Congressional Art Competition in Washington, D.C. A junior at Plenty Coups High School in Pryor, Montana, he won with a first-class pencil drawing of a Crow chief wearing a traditional headdress. Leon says: "It represents the chiefs in our Crow culture. The feathers of the war bonnet are important to me because they represent accomplishments and I want to accomplish much in my life."

Of course, not all Crow artists today create modern art. Some continue the beautiful crafts of their ancestors, such as beadwork and ceremonial

His paintings are in museums around the world, but Kevin Red Star says he will always be a student who constantly learns new ways to do his art.

Portrait by Kevin Red Star titled Crow Woman: Knows Her Medicine. *Red Star's paintings combine new artistic techniques with traditional Crow themes.*

attire. Before the Europeans came, the Crow used seeds, shells, porcupine quills, claws, bones, and stones for ornamentation. The Crow first received glass beads from other tribes who got them from the Spanish. When French trapper Francois Larouque encountered the Apsaalooke in 1805, they already were using beads to ornament clothes, riding gear, and

Before trade beads became popular, Crow women used elks' teeth to ornament their buckskin dresses.

containers. The original style of Crow beadwork was geometric designs. When the Cree entered Montana in the late 1800s, they introduced flower designs to the Crow. Beadwork is a major art form among all the Indians in Montana today.

Mary Lou Big Day is known for making traditional dolls. She was born on the Crow Reservation, and her grandmother and parents taught her many of her people's traditions. At age sixteen, she married; her husband's father was a Sun Dance leader, so his family needed to help provide financial support to allow him to serve his people spiritually. Mary Lou's mother-in-law taught her how to do beadwork, how to make moccasins and clothing the old way, and how to dry and store meats. Years later, when Mary Lou was looking for a way to help her grandson make some pocket money, she showed him how to make traditional dolls. They sold quickly, and she continued making the dolls after her grandson went to college.

Years ago, dolls were given to young girls in the Crow Tribe. These dolls taught them about a woman's responsibilities: caring for children and for elders. The dolls' bodies are sewn out of leather. Horsehair is used for the hair. Intricate beadwork and paint made from natural materials complete

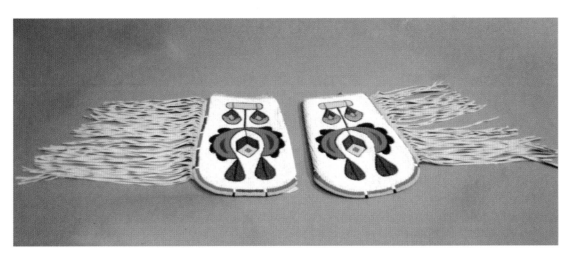

Beaded dance gloves. Flower designs made with tiny seed beads were popular with the Crow in the late 1800s.

Contemporary Arts 69

Crow girls—and Crow horses—still wear traditional outfits for special occasions.

Art for a Child's Start

In 1972, Gary Johnson came home from the hospital, a newborn baby snuggled in a beautifully beaded cradleboard. His father, Gary Senior, an artist known for his beadwork, made the cradleboard for his newborn son. Cradleboards were once used by mothers to carry their children on their backs or on horses when the Crow camps moved to follow bison herds.

For twenty-nine years, Gary Junior kept his cradleboard as a family heirloom and reminder of Crow tradition. Then, Gary Junior and his wife Lisa welcomed a daughter into the world. Their newborn, named Quinley, came home from the hospital—you guessed it—in that same beautiful cradleboard. Gary Junior hopes his daughter will someday use it for her baby.

Reported in the Billings Gazette.

the dolls' decoration. Mary Lou says, "Through my dolls, I hope to preserve our heritage for my children, grandchildren, and great grandchildren."

Whether today's Crow artists create modern music and paintings or traditional beadwork and dolls, in one way or another they all express their people's heritage through their creativity. Music, artwork, and crafts show the world something of what it means to be Crow.

Barney Old Coyote, Jr. has lived a remarkable life.

Chapter 7

The Crow's Contributions to the World

The Crow Indians have a long tradition of serving the United States, as well as their own tribal nation, with honor. Barney Old Coyote Jr. is one man who exemplifies this trait. His proud daughter, Edwina "Winnie" Old Coyote-Melkus, has recorded the story of his life.

Barney was born in 1923 into the Whistle Clan, the son of Barney Old Coyote Sr. and Mae Takes Gun. His father's clan, the Piegan, was his "teasing" clan (see chapter 4). His mother's sister Susie had been stricken repeatedly with grief—eight of her children had died—so Mae gave Barney Jr. to Susie and her husband Al to raise. This meant Barney was then adopted into the Big Lodge clan. He was named White Buffalo Calf, the name of a chief well noted for bravery. This child was blessed with the honor of several powerful names.

On December 7, 1941, Barney heard on his radio of the infamous attack on Pearl Harbor. He immediately tried to persuade his brother Hank to join the army with him. At Billings, the recruiter tried to turn away Barney from the armed services since he was only seventeen. The recruiter sent him with a paper for his parents to sign and said, "Do your parents even know how to write?" Barney replied, "Would you prefer this written in Crow or English?"

Al and Susie refused to sign the papers. So did Barney Sr. But Barney Jr. was insistent. Finally, Mae wrote a letter to the Army asking if both of her sons could join together and look out for each other. The Army agreed, and the two brothers were top of their class in basic training.

While they served in the Air Force, Barney sank a German U-boat from his A-20 aircraft off the coast of Africa. Back in Crow Country, Joe Hill heard of Barney's success and went around singing praise songs and literally waking up people from sleep to tell them of Barney's achievement. Shortly after this, the Chairman of the Crow Tribe, Robert Yellowtail (who happened to be their uncle) sent a letter to the Air Force. He requested they keep Barney and Henry in the thick of battle, so they could "count coup."

Barney and Hank flew many missions with the 97th Bomb Group. The famous general James Doolittle requested them for a particular mission. He wanted Barney to use the Crow language when messages had to be sent in code. (This was before the Navajo became famous for using the same technique in the Pacific during the war.)

On one occasion, the commander of Barney's group told his men there was a very dangerous mission to be fought. The commander said he would go and asked if anyone else would volunteer to accompany him. Barney did. At 30,000 feet (9,144 meters), amid a beautiful blue sky while the mission's planes droned along peacefully, Barney was in the machine gun turret atop his B-17 bomber. Out of nowhere, Barney heard a voice speaking to him in Crow: "Look up!"

He knew no one else on that plane knew Crow. Mystified, he did look up and saw an enemy plane diving out of the clouds to shoot them. He quickly turned his gun upward and beat the enemy pilot to the draw. The mission was saved—along with the lives of eight men in his bomber. After they returned, Barney's commander asked how he knew to look up when he did. Barney told him about the voice. The commander chuckled and said, "I like your ancestors more and more!"

As their mother had hoped, Barney and Hank looked out for each other during the war. Before combat, they would paint each other. Their flight suits hid the paint, but the commander knew about it. At night, they would recite to each other the stories they had heard from their elders as children. They came home as honored victorious warriors. Their bravery and skills had contributed to U.S. success in World War II.

After the war, Barney continued to serve the United States and the Crow Nation. He went to college, then became superintendent for the Bureau of Indian Affairs. He was Special Assistant to the Secretary of the Interior during President Lyndon B. Johnson's term. Barney founded the first Indian-owned and operated bank—the American Indian National Bank in Washington, D.C. He also was professor at Montana State University in Bozeman, where he began their Native American Studies Program. He was a key writer of the American Indian Religious Freedom Act, which was passed in 1978.

In 1988, the Veteran's Association contacted Barney, informing him that he and his brother would receive the prestigious National Award Medal. Unfortunately, Hank had just died ten days previously, and Barney was in mourning. When a Crow is in mourning, he does not partake in any celebrations. Barney's clan brother offered him a sacred pipe, however, releasing him from mourning to accept the honor for himself and his brother. People from the tribe came to see Barney and Hank recognized. When he looked back on all his accomplishments, Barney Old Coyote Jr. attributed his good fortune to following the Crow way.

Joe Medicine Crow is another outstanding contributor to the United States and the Crow Nation. Born on the reservation in 1913, as a little boy he loved to hear the stories of the Crow Nation's history. Even then, he knew his life mission—to record and preserve these precious traditions. He became the first Crow man to graduate from college, and he went on to earn his master's degree in *anthropology* from the University of Southern California. After graduation, he returned to Crow Country and began writing the stories of his people.

World War II interrupted his writing career. When the Army saw how intelligent he was, they wanted to make him an officer. He refused because the Crow way is to first earn honor in battle, then be promoted to leadership. Refusing that rank is one of Joe Medicine Crow's few regrets. The Army didn't think like the Crow do, and he didn't get another chance for promotion, despite an outstanding career of bravery in battle. He counted coup by taking fifty horses from an *elite* German unit.

After the war, he returned home and worked for the Bureau of Indian Affairs. After forty years of service to the Bureau, he returned to his life's mission of writing the tribe's history. He frequently lectures about Crow culture and history at Little Big Horn College and abroad. In 1992, he published a book titled *From the Heart of Crow Country*. This book gives the reader a fascinating excursion into the old ways of the Apsaalooke.

Within Crow Country, Joe Medicine Crow is known as a highly respected elder. To the outside world, he is a recognized historian and scholar. He has preserved the precious traditions of the Apsaalooke and shared this wealth with the outside world.

Although both Barney Old Coyote Jr. and Joe Medicine Crow have contributed a great deal to our world, it may be that the most important achievement of the Crow Nation in the past decade is not an individual achievement but the accomplishment of a highly dedicated group—Little Big Horn College. In his book, *Killing the White Man's Indian*, Fergus Borde-

Joe Medicine Crow, the outstanding Crow historian.

Dr. David Yarlott began as a student and is now the president of Little Big Horn College.

wich writes: "In a number of respects, schools like Little Big Horn and the twenty-three other tribal colleges around the country represent the most hopeful single development in Indian Country today." Little Big Horn College is even more amazing considering the way it began.

In 1982, the two-year college had just thirteen students who met in a trailer. The trailer was also shared with the Head Start program. That same year, the tribal government moved out of the building they had occupied for years and left the old building abandoned. The doors were falling off their hinges, windows were broken, and dogs wandered in and out of the building. David Yarlott, who was a student at the time, had the bright idea of going to the tribal office and asking if the college could use the old building.

When he went in to speak with the tribal chairman and several council members sitting with the chairman, they all laughed out loud when he made his request. "What would you want with that broken-down old building?" they asked. It was basically a barn at that point, and dogs and

Due to the dedication of its staff, Little Big Horn College has achieved amazing success despite scarce resources.

horses had left manure on the floor. The officials kept laughing, but they granted David use of the building and said, "Good luck."

That same year, a new president of the college had been hired, Janine Pease Windy Boy. David approached her with his idea. She said, "Are you sure we really have that old building?" She made a few calls and it was confirmed, so they started making the move.

When they first moved in, everything looked dismal, but the new president caught the same vision David had. They didn't just look at the manure, the broken windows, the falling doors—they saw a vision of what the building could be. David, his wife Deborah, three other staff members,

President Windy Boy, and seven students rolled up their sleeves and started to clean up the mess. The Bureau of Indian Affairs assisted some. At first they held classes in the gym area with partitions between them. When it rained, students and instructors just worked around the drips.

David Yarlott worked as the activities director and coach. He was paid only $200 per semester and eventually left for another job. Throughout its history, Little Big Horn College has operated on a shoestring budget. The entire faculty receives in salaries less than most departments get in other schools. They have half as much per capita to spend on each student as do state schools. Given what they have materially, the accomplishments of Little Big Horn College are all the more remarkable.

Janine Pease Windy Boy worked hard for

> "Without the White Man's education you are his victim, with it you are his equal."
>
> —*the words of Chief Plenty Coup, spoken a century ago*

Dale Old Horn teaches Crow language and culture at Little Big Horn College. He is a nationally sought-after powwow master of ceremonies.

more than a decade to increase the school's enrollment, faculty, and courses. In 1990, she was named Indian Educator of the Year, and in 1994 won the prestigious MacArthur Foundation Award. Enrollment at the college grew from dozens to hundreds. Tribal politics did not always make the job easy, and at a raucous council meeting in January of 2001, she was removed from office.

In 1997, David Yarlott returned to the college, now as Dr. David Yarlott, having earned his doctorate in education. He was teaching at the school in 2001 and was hired to serve as the president of the college.

Currently, the school's enrollment is three hundred. That may seem small, but the school has a fabulous success rate. Students who go from Little Big Horn College to four-year colleges are sixty times more likely to be successful than those Indian students who go straight from high school. Construction has begun on a new and vastly improved campus. Yet the

A sign shows plans for the new Little Big Horn College.

Little Big Horn College did an amazing job teaching students in a formerly abandoned building. Faculty and students look forward to completion of this vastly improved campus.

most important and unique aspect of the school's success is not seen in numbers. The kind of education it offers sets Little Bighorn apart from thousands of other community colleges. Here, students can take courses in the Crow language. They can also take classes with titles like: Crow Thought and Philosophy, Crow Oral Literature, Crow History, and Music and Dance of the Crow.

For centuries, education has been used as a means of "blending" people into sameness. Indian schools established by the Indian Affairs Department were designed to "kill the Indian in order to save the child." Now, when the Crow people administer and teach at their own college, Apsaalooke culture is nourished and preserved rather than squelched by higher education. Crow *philosophy* and art are being encouraged at the college, which not only strengthens the tribe but enriches all of America.

Little Bighorn Casino is Crow Nation tribal enterprise. The casino features a hundred slots and a restaurant.

Chapter 8

Challenges for Today, Hopes for Tomorrow

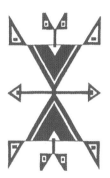

Today, Jared Stewart has a full life. He has his own family, a musical career, and responsibilities as newly elected tribal council member. In a way, all these positive things were inspired by a tragedy, Jared's little brother was shot in the head. That tragic event made Jared want to live twice as hard, giving life all he can. Losing his brother made him see how special life is and gave him the desire to make the most out of every single minute. Wrestling good outcomes from dire circumstances—that's a theme common to many Crow people.

Dale Old Horn of Little Big Horn College has pointed out: "Because of the loss of culture, many of the practices of the Apsaalooke people are being replaced by a tremendous amount of dysfunctional behavior, such as alcohol abuse, drug abuse, spouse abuse, child abuse, gambling addictions." After centuries of being pushed down by non-Indian society, a disheartening amount of suffering exists in the Crow Nation. One estimate says 40 percent of adults on the reservation have problems with alcohol. Driving fatalities are just one horrendous effect of drug and alcohol abuse.

Underlying other social ills is the problem of poverty. Since the Fort Laramie Treaty of 1851, the U.S. federal government has allowed outside interests to steal, buy, or make use of Crow Nation resources. Economically, more has been taken than given back to the Crow. As a result, there are too few good jobs in Crow Country. One estimate says unemployment on the Crow Nation is a devastating 85 percent. When people lack jobs, depression, drug or alcohol dependence, and other problems are more likely to become lifestyle patterns.

Loss of traditional ways of living has also hurt people's physical health. As Dale Old Horn writes in *Apsaalooke Social and Family Structure*:

> The government supplies food through health programs which is high in fat, starch, and sugar which leads many Apsaalooke to develop diabetes. A lot of Apsaalooke people are having to go to dialysis every two days, many are suffering from eyesight loss, some of them are suffering from kidney failure due to diabetes. It is a lifestyle that was brought on through dependency, through loss of pride, through subjugation which is killing not only the culture but the Apsaalooke themselves.

The Crow land itself faces challenges to its health. As one official report says:

> In 1996, Tribal environmental staff identified surface water contamination from an upstream wastewater treatment plant and septic systems contaminating surface water used as a drinking water source and as a water source for sweat lodges as the major reservation environmental problem which may be hazardous to the health of reservation residents.

Perhaps the most serious threat to the Apsaalooke is not physical but cultural. The importance of Indian nations keeping their languages alive cannot be overstated. Scholars say that if people lose their language, they will also lose more than half of their culture. How can you learn ideas and practices if you no longer have the words to describe them? For more than a hundred years, federal Indian policy worked deliberately to make Indians stop speaking their own tongue. Dale Old Horn says,

Language education beginning in Head Start classes will help revitalize the Apsaalooke language.

A good example of the effects of Euro-American society upon the Apsaalooke is with native language usage. Historically, one hundred percent of all Apsaalooke spoke the Apsaalooke language. In 1989 a survey was conducted in the grade schools on or near the reservation, and roughly thirty-three percent of Apsaalooke children under the age of ten spoke the Apsaalooke language.

Among the Crow, however, there is some reason to be encouraged. William Bryan, in *Montana's Indians*, writes: "The Crow people have one of the highest rates of native language retention in the country. Some of the reasons for this success are that the Crow reservation never had boarding schools, the clan system remains a strong part of Crow culture, Crow people still speak Crow at almost all social events." Little Big Horn College and other tribal institutions are working hard to preserve the Apsaalooke language.

For any nation, children are the ones who hold the keys to a better tomorrow. Crow youth today show great promise for the future. Lucretia Birdinground, for example, is a tenth grader attending St. Labre Catholic School on the Northern Cheyenne reservation. She is a member of the

Lucretia Birdinground, one of the award-winning Rez Protectors, looks to the future with bright hopes.

Crow Nation but lives at St. Labre during the week, going home on week-ends. Two years ago, when Lucretia was in the eighth grade, she attended Pretty Eagle Catholic School in the town of St. Xavier on the Crow Reservation. She made friends with the other three girls in her grade: Omney Sees The Ground, Brennet Stewart, and Kimberly Deputee. One day the science teacher and coach, Mr. Jack Joyce, talked with each girl individually and told of an exciting national science competition. Teams around the country would be competing. The object was to look around the community, find a problem, and solve it. The girls decided to become a team.

The girls looked around the Crow Reservation and saw that one problem affecting many people was the lack of affordable housing. Crow families may be crowded in with several other families in a single house. Many people on the reservation can't find jobs but don't want to move away from family members. The girls interviewed family members who lived in crowded situations. They discovered that one of the problems with being so crowded was that the children had a hard time doing homework because of the noise around them.

With the problem identified, the girls had to come up with a solution—how to build affordable housing. First, they decided on a name for themselves: the Rez Protectors. Next, they thought about what was available on the reservation. With a little prompting from their science teacher, they realized a lot of hay was grown in the area. Mr. Joyce let them know that there was a way to build houses out of hay bales covered with a stucco mixture of lime, sand, and cement.

Many of the people the girls talked to about the hay bale idea were skeptical. Wouldn't water, heat, or cold leak in? Wouldn't a spark of fire set the whole house blazing? The girls undertook a series of tests to determine *feasibility*. Tests with a torch and thermometer showed the bales were unaffected by heat and resistant to fire. A thorough soaking showed them to be entirely water resistant.

With the hay and stucco bales having passed all the tests, the girls wrote a ten-page paper stating the problem, the proposed answer, the test procedure, and results. They also had to tell contest officials what they would do with the $25,000 dollars they might win. The girls decided they would spend the money on a straw building study hall for Crow students. This would give kids from crowded houses a place to study and be an example of what such a building would look like.

Over five hundred applicants joined the contest from all over the country. The top ten teams would get to go to Orlando, Florida, to spend a week at the Disney World Resort. In March, Mr. Joyce was notified that the girls

No Good-byes

"There is no word for "Good-bye" in Crow . . . they say, "See you later."
—*Winnie Melkur*

Four eighth-grade students from Pretty Eagle Catholic School in St. Xavier won a $25,000 grant to benefit their community in the Bayer National Science Foundation Competition. Showing their project at the finals at Walt Disney World, Florida, are (from left to right) Coach Jack Joyce, Omney Sees The Ground, Brennet Stewart, Lucretia Birdinground, and Kimberly Deputee.

had made it to the top thirty winning teams. One day in April, as the girls were starting their school day, Mr. Joyce told them that this was the day he would be getting a call to let them know if they had made it to the top ten teams. When Mr. Joyce was called to the office for a phone call, the girls waited nervously. He returned with good news: the Rez Protectors were one of the ten teams chosen.

In June, the team and Mr. Joyce went to Florida. The girls had a very good time with the other students. Everyone had excellent projects. Many of the other kids told the Rez Protectors they hoped they won. One at a time, the groups presented their projects to the judging board. On the last day, awards were given for various categories at a special banquet. The Rez Protectors wore their Crow traditional dresses for their presentation and were given the best dressed award. At the end of the banquet, the announcement was made that the teams had been waiting for . . . the Rez Protectors were first-place winners!

The hay bale study hall was built not too long after the girls returned to the reservation. Mr. Joyce put the girls in touch with Robert Young, who has a group called the Red Feather Development Group. Robert visited the Crow Reservation and sat down with the team to develop blueprints for the study room. He solicited volunteers on the Internet to help with the building project. He needed fifty volunteers—but five times that offered to help! The building is now completed and being used as a study space.

Several fun opportunities presented themselves later on for the girls. Oprah Winfrey had them on her show. They were interviewed for the *Today Show* and by Tom Brokaw, and they were invited to Al Gore's Family Reunion Conference where Lucretia spoke on stage to five hundred people.

Today, Lucretia speaks fondly of gratitude to her family for their encouragement, not only for this project but also all along life's way. Her grandfa-

The Rez Protectors Team.

The future of the Crow Nation is its children—like these at the Boys & Girls Club.

ther, Glen Birdinground, has had a profound influence on her. He spent many years in a wheelchair, but that didn't stop him from becoming a tribal judge. He always encouraged Lucretia and her little brother to make good choices in life and to stay away from alcohol. Before he died in 2000, he adopted both Lucretia and her brother as his children. Lucretia wants to honor her grandfather and the rest of her family by working hard and being successful. Her future desire is to go to college and become a lawyer.

The hopes of the Crow tribe rely on young people such as Lucretia. Throughout the centuries, natural forces, hostile tribes, and an unscrupulous government have threatened the Crow people. Constantly under pressure, they have endured. They have learned when to form partnerships and when to fight, how to be both progressive and traditional. The Crow today face many challenges, but they do so with a long track record of success in the face of opposition.

"Baleeliikukuash Ahomuuk."
"Thank you for listening to us."

Further Reading

Bryan, William L., Jr. *Montana's Indians Yesterday and Today*. Helena, Mon.: American & World Geographic Publishing, 1996.

Colton, Larry. *Counting Coup: A True Story of Basketball and Honor on the Little Big Horn*. New York: Warner Books, 2000.

Medicine Crow, Joseph. *From the Heart of Crow Country*. Lincoln: University of Nebraska Press, 2000.

Medicine Crow, Joseph. *Brave Wolf and Thunderbird: Tales of the People*. New York: Abbeville Press, 1998.

Old Horn, Dale D., and Timothy P McCleary. *Apsaalooke Social and Family Structure*. Crow Agency, Mon.: Little Big Horn College Press, 1995.

For More Information

Chief Plenty Coup State Park Official Web Site
www.nezperce.com/pcmain.html

Crow Tribe Community Profile
www.mnisose.org/profiles/crow.htm

Little Big Horn Battlefield
www.nps.gov/libi/

Little Big Horn College
www.lbhc.cc.mt.us/

Welcome to Crow Country
www.angelfire.com/my/rabiddeputydawg/main.html

Publisher's Note:

The Web sites listed on this page were active at the time of publication. The publisher is not responsible for Web sites that have changed their address or discontinued operation since the date of publication. The publisher will review and update the Web sites upon each reprint.

Glossary

accountability: The willingness to accept responsibility.

advocates: Those who defend or stands up for another or a belief.

anthropology: The study of human beings.

bustles: A framework that expands and drapes the back of an outfit.

cavalry: An army made up of soldiers on horseback, in airplanes, helicopters, or motor vehicles.

constitution: The basic rules or laws of a nation or other organized group.

controversy: A discussion characterized by opposing views.

criteria: A set of standards on which a decision is based.

cultural oppression: The restriction of the practice of a group's rituals and beliefs.

diverse: Having different characteristics.

ecstatic: The state of having overwhelming joy.

elite: The best of a particular class.

emcee: Master of Ceremonies. A person who acts as a host for an event, introducing performers, speakers, etc.

epic: A long poem telling the tale of a legendary historical figure.

factionalism: A group characterized by subgroups with opposing views who act for their own benefit.

feasibility: The likelihood of something being done successfully.

impressionist: An art style in which the natural world is represented through dabs of unmixed primary colors that simulate actual reflected light.

inefficiency: Being done in a wasteful manner.

ingenious: Showing intelligence, aptitude, and creativity.

metaphor: A figure of speech in which one word or phrase is used to represent something else.

New Deal: A program developed by President Franklin D. Roosevelt to promote economic recovery and social reform during the 1930s.

nomads: People with no fixed home who move from place to place, usually seasonally.

notoriously: Unfavorably known.

omnipotent: Having unlimited power or authority.

perseverance: Persistence in achieving something; "stick-to-itiveness."

peyote: A type of cactus; a drug derived from mescal buttons.

philosophy: The grounds and concepts of a belief system.

prestige: The importance in the opinions of other people.

renaissance: Rebirth.

sacramental: Having the characteristics of something associated with a religious or cultural rite; a concrete object or activity that reveals the spiritual world.

scouts: People who go ahead to explore an area, often in search of an enemy.

traditionalists: People who prefer to practice the old way of doing things.

tuberculosis: A highly contagious lung disease.

Index

═══════════════

Biographies

Kenneth McIntosh is a pastor, and his wife Marsha is a schoolteacher. They both took leave from their regular jobs to work on this series. Formerly, Kenneth worked as a junior high teacher in Los Angeles, California. He wrote *Clergy* for the Mason Crest series "Careers with Character." The McIntoshes live in upstate New York and have two children, Jonathan and Eirené. They are grateful for the opportunity this work has given them to travel and meet with many wonderful Native people.

Martha McCollough received her bachelor's and master's degrees in anthropology at the University of Alaska-Fairbanks, and she now teaches at the University of Nebraska. Her areas of study are contemporary Native American issues, ethnohistory, and the political and economic issues that surround encounters between North American Indians and Euroamericans.

Benjamin Stewart, a graduate of Alfred University, is a freelance photographer and graphic artist. He traveled across North America to take the photographs included in this series.